The Weight
of Missing

EMILY R. PAGET

THE CHOIR PRESS

First published in the United Kingdom in 2023 by
The Choir Press

ISBN 978-1-78963-355-9

ebook 978-1-78963-356-6

Contents

For all that's missing

Lost

The Missing

I imagined once
That time
In all its wisdom
Would cloak me
In forgiveness
Breathing small mercy
On sorrow's soul.
But now
All there is
Is silence
Stretched thin
And bowed
By the weight
Of all
That's
Missing.

Ghost

I am a ghost.
Erased
Like a smudge
On the page.
I fade
In the dark
Hand held out
But nothing
Is there.
Thin air
Carries my call.
I fall.
Sinking beneath
The ice
Where the silence
No longer stings
I cannot see
And all that is left
In the dark
Is me.

Ice Cold

Out of the door
I ran
Bare feet
Hitting dirt and
Earth washed
By storms.
Sky the colour
Of ice
Cold like my eyes.
I fear now
I will never
Be warm.

The Night

I am the night
Silent in breath
Counting the stars
With an ache
In my chest.
I am blinded
By smoke and mirrors
And us.
The weight of missing
Driving heart to rib
In ruthless
Pulsating thrusts.
Yet still I float
In burning hope
The winding November embers
A twisted, blackened cloak.
I am night
And I live for the dark
For those stolen moments
When I can feel
My heart.

Too Much

I think
I will always be
A little unsure
Of the light in me.
Too much hurt
And too much heart
Tilt me ever closer
Towards the dark.

The Huntress

In the hands of death
I rest.
Bone tired
Sins confessed.
A siren's solace
Is all I get
Bleeding sorrow
A restlessness.
Tonight, I meet
Once more with death.
Villainous
Heartless
Blood-soaked
Huntress.

Everything

In silent streaks
The darkness crawls
It climbs beneath my skin.
It steals my hope
With savage screams
Yes, night
Night changes
Everything.

The Broken Ones

The lost ones meet in shadows
Cast by an unforgiving sun
They seek the other broken ones
Who have spun and come undone.
And in the dark where no one sees
These souls can dance
For eternity.

Into Being

The past lives in me.
It whispers sadness
Into the dark
A soft and sacred song
That draws me in
So my body
Sings.
It creates
This deep, searing ache
In that shadowed space
Between sleep and
Steeling awake.
A place that is
Born into truth.

And if I
Let go
I am called once more
Into being
Freeing a part of my heart
Locked up tight
Intentionally veiled
And hiding from
Scrutinised sight.

At the siren's sound
The walls of silence
Crash violently down
And I am left to drown
In yearning tenderness.
Leaning and longing
Into translucent past
Where loving light
Lingers soft
In my grasp.

No Sign

I'm looking for something
Impossible to find
A stone amongst stones
A place with no sign.
And the longer I seek
The more I am lost
The smoke rising higher
Lines blurred and crossed.
And the clock doesn't wait
Time marches on
There's only this moment
No promise of beyond.

Stolen Sunset

The storm blew out its own fury
And the ashen clouds gave way
To a stolen sunset
Tucked against the horizon
Bleeding faded orange
Into heavy skies.
A slow burn
Eking out the light
Where silhouetted trees
Stand guard against
Nefarious night.

It Will Remain

I hurt in silence
Like the rain
And it's not
The same pain
But a guttural ache
That won't go away.
It stays
And here
It will remain.

Forsaken Tears

Darkness treads tight-lipped
The shadows hanging listless
On long threads of silken web.
A silence weighted by chilled bones
And trees that grieve
Their unclothed thrones.
On these numb November nights
I lie
Eyes searching coal-slashed skies
For a ghost who floats
In dark depths of
Desperate hope.
I see him waiting
Beyond the obsidian wall
Reaching that hollow
Where forsaken tears
Fall.

The Truth Lies

Night comes
Clouds closing in
To leech the light
And I cling to the shadows
With all my might.
For enemies wait
In darkened dreams
And truth is not
All that it
Seems.

Midnight Spell

I grow
Tired of waiting.
Twilight pools in silver ribbon
Stretching shadows into
Ghosts.
The press of winter's
Breath
Bleeds me silent.
A shiver kissing skin.
Shaking limbs within.
When grief sinks in
I will not tell.
For darkness sings
Her midnight spell.

Never Mine

A heart I wish was mine
Lies latent in the shadows
Balanced in that space
We create between
Dusk and dawn.
Drifting in dreams
Yet far apart
Crawling to corners
That cry out hard
To lamentable
Shameful
Scratching
Dark.

This heart is pencilled
In cloudy memories
Of intimate pleasure and
Extraordinary possibilities.
It sings low and quiet
This love divine
A haunting lullaby
Of what was never
Mine.

A Moment

I see you
In that moment
When the sun shows
What it means to shine.
And in that brief heat
We are framed by grief
The light baring our
Blackness like a canvas
Full of ghosts.
The shadow of us
Is lined with charcoal
And the sounds of snapping
Are nullified by sadness.

These colours we once held
Tight in our arms
Are now mere rainbows
In the dark.
Fleeting memories
That last no more than
A moment
Before the creeping darkness
Edges the sun to set
And our history of hurt
Lays down once more
To rest.

There's No Such Place

There's no such place
No trace of earth or bricks or stone
Nowhere that truly feels like home.
But I look
Along each turn of the path
And every crack that splits
The asphalt wide open
To engulf all that's been sewn
And grown with so much care.
The delicate parts of hope and faith
Buried in mud that leaves no trace
Of that fragile truth that felt
So
Goddamn
Safe.
And now that space is lost
In a chasm of blackened dust
And burning mistrust.
And I feel everything and nothing
All at once
And surely now I must confront
All that is wholly missing.
The weight that walks beside me
Along that path
Looking for something
That's lost
In the past.

Driving The Darkness

It feels somehow fitting
To be here alone
With only the darkness
To call my own.
It wraps me whole
And carries me in
Guarding my secrets
And soothing my sins.

Time goes slow
But silence moves
Stealing from shadows
The moonlight eludes.
I wait like a ghost
For the rising sun
Driving the darkness
I can never
Outrun.

Weighted

I am weighted
And sinking with the tide
Pulled and twisted
By sweet fate and time.
Darkness descends
And takes a hold
Heavy as stone
And twice
As cold.

Silence

In the shrill silence
That comes with dark
There is a growing feud
Between my lost parts.
They shake and wake
My resting bones
And urge me out
Where the shadows roam.
I feel the pull
Like edges of silk
Fraying and floating
In invisible guilt.
I'd like to wish
Upon a star
To keep my dreams
As tragic as they are.
But I let the silence
Take its fill
Allow the darkness
To go in
For the kill.

All That's Missing

I stare out
Into the half-light
Almost night.
A cloak of wintry
Coal-fire smoke
Pulling the day
Into long drawn out
Charcoal brush strokes.
A colourless sadness
Bleeds
As the last leaves
Fall dying to the ground.
The only sound is
Silence.
Unforgiving.
As tragic and dark
As the weight
Of all
That's missing.

Hidden

And so, it begins
The day pulling
On night's apron strings
Letting loose
The silken thread
That binds the earth
To moon's waxen web.
I feel it in the air
An absence that aches
So, when I wake from inky sleep
The weight hangs heavy
Pulling me low
So I drown in its biting undertow.
Winter's chill in icy breath
Blown and falling
Into frozen depths.
Shadows locked in brittle bones
Secrets hidden
That I am seldom
Shown.

The Fall

Fallen
I wait.
Soft measured footfalls
A saintly saving grace.
Missing.

Forgotten Tears

Gone

He is gone
And I can
No longer feel
The warmth of him.
So I find
A quiet place
To be alone
Along the riverbank
Where the curlews
Come calling
And the moonlight
Sings soft blues
Over the water.

Tears

I sit silent in the long grass
Where the banking curves blithely
And the rushes lean out
Along the water's edge.
And though I may sit
Without a sound
My eyes are never dry.
Tears hidden in the river
As I too
Hide.

Sorrow's Sun

Taken
To the edge of
Sorrow.
Heart sliced
With serrated knife
Bleeding out
Into silent night.
Then
You.
You who soothe
The bloom of tears.
Fingertips a
Feather touch
That will never be
Enough.
For sorrow's sun
Sets
And the dark
Is real.
It's all
I can ever
Really
Feel.

Lost To The Promise

I grow weary
Heavy limbed.
Lost to the promise
Of everything.
Floating in folly
Grey sheets of sin
A blanket of ghosts
To be buried in.
I sink to a silence
That pierces my skin
Bleeding black water
On paper-thin wings.

Mannequin

In these almost winter days
When the sun's rays lie low
And the sky hides in slate grey
Bruised with mauve
I grow frail and slow.
Bones brittle in frozen breath
And heartbeat heavy
In a dance with death.
This mannequin dressed
In mourning black
Cracked and slashed with
Crushing ice
Biting back with savage spite.
Serene in the shadows
Bled stark and grim
Soothed by the darkness
That writhes within.

Rain Scented

Shadows lift like ghosts
Ceding light to kiss the stars
Rain scented secrets.

For The Light

I am
November rain.
I fall
Restlessly
And stubbornly
Unrestrained.
I am bound
By the water
And enshrined
By the sky.
Searching hollows
For the light
In my eyes.

Winter's Breath

The press of winter's breath
Spreads silent
Seeking solace in silver heights
And incantations whispered
In the waning moonlight.
Earth indelibly marked
By Sorrow's icy heart.

The Sun Sighs

The sun sighs as it sinks
To the bottom of the sky
I watch it go
Slow and graceful
Breathing golden fire.
And in the glow
It leaves
As a parting gift
My tears fall
Like silver
Spilling into the earth
To join the setting sun.

Sorrow

Sorrow pools
In the shadow of ice
A barren beauty
Of whispered white.
Skies shuttered
By silver stripes
Scattered in breath
Into softest light.

The Weight Of Everything

I shape my goodbye
Under lilac-spattered skies
Voice soft
Spoken like sorrow.
Already the clouds
Threaten to spill
Torn clean at the seams
By the weight of
Everything.
I tell my lie
As fading embers
Fly
And darkness descends
To drown me.

The Flood

Sadness
Threads through my bones
The flood of blood weighted
By a stillness of breath held close.
Plaintive.

Let Go

I know
That I must
Let it go.
Surrender
The fated
Tide of time
That pulls and
Twists to seep
Bone deep.
Let it lie.
Let it be.
Let it guide
My destiny.

Too Long

I held on
Too long.
Tangled up
In silver stardust
And a soulless moon.
Watching shadows stretch
Into callous
Gaping wounds.
Straining to
Count the breaths left
In sorrow's aching womb.
How frail that moon
And the whisper
Of my heart.
There in the stillness
Of the unremitting
Dark.

State Of Grace

I am lost
In that space.
In that
Silent
State of grace.
Sinking into shadows
Scented with rose.
Fearlessly floating
Where no one else goes.

Forgotten Tears

Sorrow
Sighs.
She is glassy
Like a pool
Plunged
In winter ice.
Forgotten tears
Fall fearlessly
Hardened into stone
Buried under skin
Through marrow
Right down to bone.

Other Half

I rest
In the carved out
Crest of a
Subtle moon.
She is soothing
In her caress
And I am left
To seek my peace
Searching the stars
For wherever
You are.

I follow the trail
Through Ursa Major
Along every layer
Of glitter and flare
But you
Are not there.

Hercules grieves
Off to the side
But he holds no signal
That you are nearby.
The strongman hero
Who never dies
Will stand here forever
Immortalised.

Draco loops his tail wide
Fiery breath
Lighting the sky
A shimmer-filled
Blazing
Impassioned sigh.

It matches my own
For I am alone
Among these myths
And legends.
Forever searching
The stars in the dark
Looking for signs
Of my soul's
Other half.

Unspoken Promise

Twin Souls

Somewhere in the dark
Where the stars riot
In fervent profusion
I wait for you.

We have never met
But our spirits pull
On invisible thread.
Joined yet far apart.

For souls sing to souls
In magnetic melody
Long before bodies
Ever meet.

A Separation

We are
A separation
Of two halves
Floating in
Permanent rotation
Of different parts.
The path of
Time and distance
Between us.

The Reply

When I am silent
The earth sighs.
And in that hushed sorrow
I hear your heart
Reply.

Broken Pieces

Paths are sometimes
Meant to cross
For broken souls
Cry out in the dark
To rise and meet
And weave their
Broken pieces together.
To smooth their jagged
Damaged edges
And find the strength
They already had
But didn't know.

That Space

I wait for you
Where the sun
No longer warms me
And the wall that stands
Between us
Casts its shadow
No more.
Up there
Like Perseus to Andromeda
The stars link our souls
And in my dreams
You are here.
I no longer have to fear
That space you leave behind you.
Up there
Talking to the moon
The nightmares cease
And I may sit
In silent reverie
Soaking up these
Precious
Midnight
Memories.

How Far

My eyes have never seen
The space that fits your dark
But I know in my heart
There lies more beauty
In the shadows
Of those forsaken parts
Than can ever last
In the glare of the sun.
Yet still we wait
For a day that never comes
And we come undone in our own
Separate time and space
Displaced by expectation
And our own fall from grace.
It must be fate
To love so hard yet
Never lie in those arms
We truly live for.
Destined only to dance in dreams
And lean into night's palm
To mend our grieving hearts.
The broken seem so strong
But no one ever tells you
How far and how deep
They have gone.

One More Day

The sun slips slow
To greet the sea
Seeping orange
Into murky black.
One more day
Has gone
And we circle sadly
Around that sun.
Set apart by stretches
Of successive lands
Luscious green
And dusty brown
And an ocean
Both vast and furious
Relentlessly pulling
Drawing us
Further apart.

Affinity

I have
A restlessness
Inside me
That moves
Like water.
A constant
Push and pull
A whirlpool
Of beginnings and ends.
But he
He stills that which
Moves inside.
So there is no pain
Of past sins
Nor agony
Of what might be.
Just a hand in the dark
And our affinity.

The Spark

I feel him
Like a spark
Lighting up
Every hollow
In the dark
His shadow
Stroking softly
On that glass
Around my heart.
He moves towards me
Gently
Like the sloping sun
At dusk.
He whispers low
And tender
Of love and faith
And trust.

Him

He was a gift
The bearer of quiet conviction
His soul spoke softly
Of integrity and grace
And a knowing
She could not shy away from.
He taught her
That not all those who wander
Are lost
And not all silence is lonely.
His whispered offering
Of benevolent peace
Felt more vital
Than any broken promise
Or strangled belief.

Her

Hers was a warmth
Like no other
As light as any feather
She was more than sunshine
And he could watch her
Rise and fall
Forever.

Unspoken Promise

Ours is a look
Of purest longing.
Of bottled green
And soft, gilded brown
Enough to drown.
An unspoken promise
Of more in our hearts
A path through the shadows
A way out of the dark.

Stealing Shadows

We lean together
Lips pressed and
Bodies blessed
By the truth
That lies between us.
And as seconds shift
And gravity persists
We draw it all
Stealing shadows
As we fall.

Sweet Sadness

I feel it
In the soft pearl
Of pale skin
And the tempered warmth
As you
Breathe it all in.
The subtle scent
Of sandalwood and citrus
And the hushed words
That are
Whispered between us.
These tender hearts and
Sonorous souls
Moving in tandem
Sweet sadness
Consoled.

Infinite Grace

In the silent sanctuary
Of your forgiving eyes
Lies a potent truth
That roots and climbs.
It breathes in hickory
Cedar and oak
Tenderly tracing
A new born hope.
With benevolent calm
Truth touches my face
Smoothing the worry
Gifting infinite grace.

Slow Burn

We are a study
In soft movement
A slow burn
Of white heat
Flecked with green.
The green of growth
And muted hope.
The way the sun rises
And changes
The look of things.
A tug of future love
The breath of feeling.
Seeking outward
Yet tethered within.
Finding strength
In all
The good
Things.

Cloaked In Hope

We stand on the corner
Hands braced and
Face-to-face
As we wait
For night to
Hold us in its shadows.
For dark to fall
And neon lights to shine
Like beacons
Through the black.
And when the dirt of day
Makes way
For night's devilry
And decay
A steady pulse
Beating long and low
Begging my soul to spill
All it knows
You draw me near
And whisper warmth
In my ear.
So as shadows shift
And city mist clings close
We are once more
Cloaked
In hope.

Only Love Can Meet The Missing

I dreamt last night
And in my dream
Your hands came out
To meet me.
And beneath the silence
Of night's ambition
I felt your breath
On the back of my neck.
Fingers caught
In gentle faith
Merge together
In aching embrace.
Two souls joining
In the depths of night
Braced for darkness
But trusting the light.
So, we let go
No longer resisting
For only love
Can meet
The missing.

If He Were Here

I am late
But I cannot care
For he talks
Softly in my ear
Of all the things
He would do
If he were here.

Since he's not
I listen hard
Slowly unfolding
In a drawn-out pace
Returning his softness
With a smile
On my face.

Butterfly's Touch

I feel it building
A pleasure to fill
Every crevice
And shadow
That grows
Beneath my skin.
A wistful
Longing
That flows through me.
An ache that waits
For no one.
Yet the rush of this
Butterfly's touch
Is never enough.
The flame now lit
And mixed with lust
Cannot be brushed away.
It builds and fills
Each part until
All that is left
To do
Is love
The hell
Out of you.

Fragile
Truth

The Gift

I watch it approach
That momentary gift of time
It floats
Sweeping upward
Bearing my hope.
Caught on a wistful wind
It spins and darts
Straight past.
I watch it go
Too slow to reach out
And grab its wispy tail.
Fleeting that space
Stretched and etched
In the shadows
Passed and now over
Yet no less crucial
In its closure.

Remembering To Forget

I sit still
In the only place
I feel even a
Touch of grace.
Silver sand
Meets grey-green sea
In great pulls
Of tidal grief.
And you
You are there with me.
We sit
In silent synchronicity.
There is melody on our breath
For together
We are remembering
To forget.

Release

I seek guidance from the sea.
The swell and shift
Of sand and salted water
Washed clean by moving tide.
The very motion
Mellowing my mind
And smoothing out
Those creases left behind.

Like waves that flatten the stones
Forever disowned and tossed to shore
I wait for signs of more.
A signal.
A redemption
To absolve me of my sins
The salt on my lips
Purging that which persists
To plague me
So, like sea glass
My sharp edges may be
Buffed and smoothed
No longer weighted by
Shadows and half-truths.

And there
Standing renewed
In translucent, unlocked calm
I open my arms
To sweet benevolent peace
Swept up grief
Tossed to the waves
And finally
Released.

Fragile Truth

This fragile truth
Hangs
On a single
Silken thread
Lilac feathered trust
Dusted in silver.
Weighted by winds
That sing
In silent prayer.
An ache found
In bruised eyes
Buried
With the pain
Forever hidden
Inside.

Gypsy

There is
A restlessness
In me.
It floats in
Silver strands
On shadows
Found
Trailing out to sea.
I am
Gypsy.
Wanderer.
Soul stitched
In sails
Compelled to drift
Until this rift
In my soul
Is sewn closed.
I surrender
To the skies
And the shifting
Tides of time
That pull and flood
And beat
In my blood.
I am gypsy
And my shadow
Calls.

Sacred Splendour

I am broken
Yet no longer lost.
Sinking as soft as
Snowflakes
To settle in the dust.
I lie
Hushed
As dawn floods
The horizon
Staying silent for
Sunlit silk
To dress me
In robes of
Sacred splendour.

I Rise

I am barely tamed fury
A golden jewel
Cast in coal black shadow.
And with a hungry heart
I rise
Like meadowsweet
From deep in the rich soil
To unfurl and bloom
With wild innocence.
Trailing my arms
Up to the sky
So I may feel
The warmth
Of the sun.

Indomitable Hope

My power lies
Not in the fire
I stoke and tend
To bloom inside me
Nor the steel
That climbs to line my back
And brace my bones.
No.
Mine is a strength
Only faith invokes
I fight with freedom
And indomitable
Hope.

The Dream

I dream
Of more than
I can see.
Of what might be.
I hold
In my mind
A picture
Yet undefined
But clear
In its hope
And the want
It invokes.

Empress

Empress.
Nurtured by sun
Spun in silver
And ivory silk.
Feathered wings
Lined with gold
Unfold
In smooth
Supple
Serenity.
I am legend.
I am fate.
I am delicate
Balanced
Grace.

It's Time

Breathless
I wait.
The moon shifting
In silver skies
Entwined in rings
Of smoke and silence.
Broken strings from
Fairy wings
Float silken in the shadows.
Stars align.
It's time.

Leave It All Behind

Twilight shines.
It pulls on my heart
And makes its mark
In all the silent spaces.
Seeping through flesh and bone
Sewn into skin so it may
Make its home.
The dark seeks my lonely parts
Begging to stay and pledging
To take my pain away.
For the moon is hungry
And it wants to taste
That brittle self-hate
I carry inside.

The witching hour swoops to scour
And devour all those fears and tears
I spill.
Yet still it haunts me.
The darkness comes to steal the sun
And I wait in the shadows
Holding on
Eyes on the sky and the dawn to come
A sign to rest and soothe my mind
The time to leave it
All
Behind.

No More Storm

And in that moment
Of solace and peace
When the wind dies
To a breath
And there is no more
Storm left
I trust my own instincts.
No more bending
To another's will
No more expectations
To fulfil.
I follow my heart
Let my soul
Make its mark
And through it all
I will rise.

Benevolent Respect

I rise
Like the dawn.
Emerging on clouds
Of pearl and white
The light lifting shadows
To hang in hallowed flight.
I shine then
With the sun
Full and bright with new breath
And a silence
Weighted
With hard-fought respect.

Close Enough

I bow under the weight
Of soft words and gentle trust
And I blush at the promise
Of grace and sweet redemption.
Through tears of tainted triumph
I lean close.
Close enough
To hope.

A Leap Of Faith

Dusk brings a coolness
That floats down like feathers.
The wind blowing gentle grace
Through soft rush and celandine.
I breathe in this peace
A moment of undiluted beauty
Like a benediction
For my coming
Leap of faith.

Silent Stand

And the moon
In all its wisdom
Turns the tides
Of fervent longing
To hang in lofty
Luminous humour
In the night sky.
A silent stand
Against encroaching
Dark.

I Hide My Fear In The Ocean

Sadness drives sadness
And sometimes
I am lost to it.
It breaks me like the waves
That beat into the shore
Stirring up the sands of
Sins past and lost time.
So I hide my fear in the ocean
Disguising the path of tears.
Salt mixed with salt
To clean the dirt out.
I am never cleansed
But the water soothes
That fire burning inside
And as I tumble in the surf
I surrender to
Soft chaos
Allowing the darkness in
To pick apart the sorrow.

A Guide

Daydreams filter
Like sunlight shifting
Through trees.
Marks etched and left
To stretch and heat
In each beat
Of sunlit kiss.
Woven by wisps of
Wind and fallen feathers
To stir and stroke
That sliver of hope
And guide it
Through the darkness.

Never Too Late

I stand on the bridge
Soft grey cardigan
Wrapped close and fisted
Tightly at my heart.
I watch the river
In constant motion
Smoothing stones as it flows
And as the shadows grow
I lift my arms
To feel the weighted air
Of twilight
Eyes closed
I smile at the promise
Of a new day to come.
For life is full
Of second chances
And it's never too late
To start over.

Divine

I watch
As fire ignites
Flying great sparks
Into the night sky
And for those seconds
The embers dance
To join the stars
As lit as they are
Like glitter against the dark.
Silhouetted trees loom large
As if on guard against the shadows
And I
I am calm.
The night holds promise
Poised on its lips
And I will not resist
Its pull.
For though I seek
The light and warmth of sun
I come undone when darkness thrums
Its heady beat on silent drum.
Yes, I am life.
I am light.
But I am also
Divinely dark.

Wildfire

I am wildfire from hell
No longer quiet
But lit by a thousand suns.
I am spun from
Blackened thread
Wound tight to choke.
I stoke my own
Burning embers
To rise like smoke
From the ash
And float to the sky
No matter the lies
And bitter denial
I will suffer the blow.
So come on.
Ready.
Set.
Let's go.

Never Doused

I am light
Bleeding colour.
A kaleidoscope of
Warring dyes
That rule in
Painted pools
Of pure fire
In my eyes.
I ride my fate
On waves of
Tinted fury.
Vivid hues of fuchsia
Green and blue
A multi-coloured tide
That seethes and writhes
Inside my mind.
So here I lie
With that fire
In my eyes
And I will not be put out
No matter how much
I am
Doused.

CPSIA information can be obtained
at www.ICGtesting.com
Printed in the USA
BVHW032208270223
659375BV00002B/12

9 781789 633559